SOAR TO LEADERSHIP SUCCESS

Lead YOUR Team Like an Aviator

By Ramon Ware

Copyright 2023 by Ramon Ware – All rights reserved.

It is not legal to reproduce, duplicate, or transmit any part of this document in either electronic means or printed format. Recording of this publication is strictly prohibited.

Paperback ISBN 979-8-9851015-3-9

RW Leadership Coaching LLC
San Jose, CA 95160

This book is dedicated to:

My wife, Elaine, who is not only my chief editor but also my most ardent supporter, always urging me to pursue my dreams. Every day with you is more fulfilling than I ever imagined, and I cherish every moment we share together. The best part of my day is being with you, and I cannot fathom a life without you by my side. My children are my constant source of inspiration, motivating me to strive to be the best version of myself. To my eldest, Desiree, who is an exceptional mother to our granddaughter, Caroline. To Simone, who, like me, is an eternal optimist and was my initial editor for this book. To Julie and Billy, "the twins", who remind me that we are stronger when we complement each other's weaknesses with our strengths. To Andre, my youngest son, who challenges me to be a wiser and more experienced father. To Katie, who demonstrates the strength of perseverance in the face of adversity. This book is also dedicated to my departed parents, James and Marie, who left this world too soon, and my sister, Tonja, who inspires me with her perseverance and determination. To whom much is given, much is required (Luke 12:48). My family gives me way more than I could ever give back. I just pray that when my days are done, they will remember me as someone who left it all on the playing field for them.

Table of Contents

Introduction

Thunderstorms are one of the most dangerous weather events that aviators encounter. When encountering thunderstorms, aviators will either chart a course around the storm or climb to higher altitudes to avoid the turbulence. Similarly, in life, when faced with obstacles, you must either navigate around or rise above the obstacle to achieve success. In my coaching, I categorize business owners in one of three categories. The first category is the Tactical Owner. Tactical Owners are intimately involved in every detail of their business and are the chief decision-maker for everything. Solopreneurs are by nature tactical owners because they do not have employees. If you have employees but feel like your employees avoid making even the slightest decisions, you are a Tactical Owner. The second category is the Absentee Owner. If you are fortunate enough that you can afford to hire someone to run your business for you, so you do not have to actively participate in the business, you are an Absentee Owner. The third and

final category is the Strategic Owner.
Strategic Owners have built a system for
their business to run on that enables
employees to have clear lines of
authority. A Strategic Owner does not
have to be physically present all the
time but is still tuned in to the
employees and what is going on in their
business. They differ from an Absentee
Owner by their level of committed
involvement in the process. Strategic
Owners will have those crucial
conversations with their employees and
will develop and demonstrate the

company's culture. This book is for those Strategic Owners and Executives who are actively setting the strategic direction of their business and actively involved in those plans coming to fruition. To succeed, Strategic Owners and Executives need to harmonize 3 main forces: energy, motivation, and environment, just like an aviator. The actions needed to counteract and manipulate these three forces are akin to those employed by aviators to takeoff, maneuver, and land an airplane.

You can utilize this new perspective to identify areas where these forces are not in harmony and are thereby hindering your progress. By employing effective countermeasures, you can reach your goals both more efficiently and effectively. Flying by the seat of your pants may work occasionally, but a successful aviator understands the underlying forces at play and makes life-saving adjustments based on that knowledge. This book provides a framework for impactful adjustments based on this same insider knowledge, allowing you to make more informed business saving decisions. The author draws on personal experience as an aviator and graduate of the United States Air Force Academy to offer a unique perspective on how to recognize when these forces are blowing you off course so you can improve your results. If you know of someone struggling in their business, share this book with them, as it offers a different approach to decision-making that can facilitate the achievement of their business goals. The forces and countermeasures discussed apply not only to leadership roles in organizations and teams but also to life. By learning to pilot your life, business, and career effectively, you can reach new heights of success.

PART I: What is Success?

Here's the beauty of life in the United States of America: <u>YOU get to determine your own definition of success</u>. That's right, your definition of success is determined by you and that definition may change over time. As life happens, you should constantly reassess your definition of success which is a key component of a growth mindset. According to Elaine Elliott-Moskwa, PhD, and author of The Growth Mindset Workbook, there are two mindsets: Fixed and Growth. "The fixed mindset belief is that you have a certain amount of an ability or attribute – perhaps high, perhaps low – and that there is little that you can do to change this. The growth mindset belief is that although you may start with a particular level of ability or attribute, you can increase your ability or develop your attribute." Therefore, under the growth mindset, there are no limits to what you can accomplish if you focus on development of your abilities or attributes that will lead you to success.

Alternatively, under a fixed mindset, your success is predetermined, which is very limiting.

As a young adult I dreamt of success, but I never really thought about defining what success would look like for me. I thought success was a family, a house, an annual vacation, and money in the bank, i.e., the American Dream. I spent a large part of my life dreaming, wanting, and striving to be what others defined as a success. When I first arrived at the United States Air Force Academy (USAFA), success for me was redefined as graduating. As graduation approached, success was again redefined to being an aviator in the United States Air Force. Although, I arrived at USAFA without any idea of what I wanted to do in the United States Air Force, over the course of four years, the USAFA culture instilled in me a desire to be an aviator because that was what the culture was designed to produce. I am quite sure I am not the only graduate who succumbed to the cultural norm that to be a success in the United States Air Force, you had to become an aviator. Now, it all seems silly, especially since so many of my classmates went on to achieve great success as high-ranking officers in the military or highly compensated corporate executives without having become aviators. Very few young adults know what they want to do with the rest of their lives after school, so they model what accomplished adults in their sphere have done. One of my biggest regrets is that I did not take the time to fully explore other career paths or opportunities to find my own center of expertise. I always enjoyed my psychology classes; what if I had become a world-renowned psychologist? Regrettably, no one will ever know because I let my environment define success for me.

The Oxford Languages Dictionary defines success as the accomplishment of an aim or purpose. Therefore, when I work with people on how to define success for themselves, I start with a simple visioning exercise. Most visioning is focused on one single aspect of your life, such as your career or your business. However, your life is multi-dimensional, and each dimension impacts the other. You are a complex being, so you need to envision your whole self. The results of this visioning exercise represent the elephant that you want to eat. Your objectives, goals, strategies, tactics, and measures represent the breakdown of those bites that you will take to eat that elephant. The three dimensions of my visioning exercise are (1) health, (2) relationships, and (3) career/business.

Health. What does healthy look like to

you? For example, healthy for me looks like a physically strong and confident man who can stand tall as he addresses large audiences in his workshops. Also, he is a spiritual person who routinely relaxes his mind, soul, and spirit so he can operate at high levels of stress. When thinking through the answer to this question, there are multiple sub-dimensions that you can touch on, such as your spiritual health, your physical health, and your mental health. I do not want to project my beliefs onto you, which is why I encourage you to envision your own representation of what a healthy life looks like to you. Your health vision is truly your own creation, so have fun with it. For some, it may look like participating in a marathon while for others, a healthy vision of life includes yoga, practicing your religious beliefs, or other general wellness therapies. It must reflect your priorities because if you do not own it, you will not be willing to take the necessary steps to work toward your vision. This is a tough question to answer, especially if it is your first time responding. Most people will ramble as they search for the answer which is a good thing because rambling allows the brain to kick into action and helps you organize your thoughts. Oftentimes, when I speak out loud, I will catch myself saying something and realize that it sounds rather, for lack of a different word, stupid. That's when I gain clarity of thought. Tough questions are the ones that help you develop your own framework from which to improve your current circumstance. Once the answer to the above question is given, I ask the client to paint me a picture using their words of what they mean. It can be a person reading a bible or an athlete running a race; it doesn't matter, it's your picture. Your health provides you with the energy to achieve your targeted success so it is important for you to define your health priorities so you can build that energy in the most efficient way. Finally, be gracious to yourself when identifying what health looks like to you.

Relationships. What relationships are most important in your life? For some, it's family and for others it may be their friends or their clients. Regardless of your answer, good relationships give you the fuel and the motivation to weather the storms in life. In October of 2020, I was terminated from my job due to the pandemic. If it had not been for the support of my wife, I never would have left my employee mindset to pursue my dreams of becoming a business owner. She doubled down on our relationship and if I had not built up a strong emotional bank account with her, that would have been hard for her to do. In times where you do not feel that you can go on, your relationships will carry you across the finish line, which is why you must prioritize investing in people just as you would in any other investment account. Relationships take time to build, therefore their currency is defined in time. The more time you spend getting to know someone and they you, one of two outcomes becomes likely: (1) you will grow to trust each other, or (2) you will lose trust in each other. Obviously, you want to build a lot of trust in your relationships because the need for withdrawals often happens when least expected. Relationships also have a strong impact on your future. For example, most parents envision their child growing up to be a healthy, happy adult. I have never met a parent who envisioned their child growing up to be a mass murderer or serial rapist. My mother always envisioned both my sister and I graduating from college. She would speak to us in terms of "when you get your college diploma, you will…". Her words were a foregone conclusion, so it was safe for us to envision that future for ourselves as well. Well, her vision of a better life for her kids came to fruition for both my sister and me. Her vision was so powerful that I did the same for my kids and they all have college degrees. Now, a college degree does not guarantee success, however I hope those early adulting years equipped them with the ability to think for themselves and develop the resiliency needed to go after what they want. It's important for you to identify those relationships that will help you achieve success and invest in them with a high priority.

Career/Business. When you began your current career/business, what did success look like to you? Paint me a picture with your words. Have you achieved that vision? If so, what does success look like moving forward? If not, what is needed for you to achieve that original vision of success? A sub-dimension of career/business is financial. You go to work, have a career, or you own a business to get the financial resources to support your health and your relationships. I am not a fan of the "where do you see yourself in 5 to 10 years from now" question during interviews because the answer can be limiting to one dimension. You must incorporate the other dimensions of health and relationships to answer this question more accurately. When you think of the hours it will take to run your business, you should instinctively think about how those hours will be stripped away from your important personal relationships and will be spent building other relationships that expand your network. Your vision of health must be a part of the picture, such as the vacations your efforts will enable you to take and provide you with the financial resources to give to the charities of your choice.

Looking back on my life and the choices I made, I could have saved myself a lot of stress, anxiety, and depression if I had routinely taken the time to define success for myself along the way. That's why in my coaching practice, one of my most crucial questions to ask my clients is to define what success is to them at this moment in time. I now understand the transitory nature of success, which is something that I wish someone had explained to me earlier in my life. Rick Franzo is The Growth Coach of the Poconos and author of <u>How Horseshoes Saved My Life: A Tale of Two Brain Tumors</u>. In the summer of 2009, Rick went from working a full-time job and being a seasonal ski patrol officer to being diagnosed with two brain tumors and having to relearn how to walk. Rick will tell you himself that his definition of success quickly changed from day to day as he completed his rehab. Focusing

on his daily successes was the key to

him learning to walk again. Now, Rick

runs a thriving business coaching

practice and helps many business

owners get focused on their vision.

Question 2: How do You achieve Success?

Success is achieved by taking our Big Hairy Audacious Goals (BHAGs) and breaking them down into small bite sized pieces that enable us to sustain our focus. Once you achieve clarity on your current definition of success, you should spend a fair amount of time breaking that vision into smaller bites that can be accomplished in short time frames. Nothing breeds success like success, because being successful is a state of mind. Admiral William H. McRaven, a

Navy SEAL, summed up this concept in his 2014 commencement address to the University of Texas at Austin which went viral on social media: "If you want to change the world, start off by making your bed." You make your bed first thing every morning because regardless of what happens that day, you will have started it with one successful task. Admiral McRaven went on to explain that making your bed also reinforces the fact that little things matter. "If you can't do the little things right, you will never do the big things right." Success is a byproduct of our daily habits, the little things. I often ask my clients; how do you eat an elephant? The answer: one bite at a time. The reasoning behind this question is to get you to break down your BHAG into small daily habits. If you do not complete those small bites, you will never finish eating the elephant because you will get frustrated with your lack of progress or get distracted with the unimportant task(s) of the day. However, if you are hitting your small bite goals, you'll be too busy celebrating your successes on your way to conquering your BHAG.

Another reason to focus on the small

bites is that if things change, you can

quickly adjust without losing a large

investment in time.

If achieving success is as simple as

breaking our BHAGs into smaller

pieces, then why do so many people fail

to achieve their wanted success. Simple,

we lose focus. In <u>Stolen Focus: Why You</u>

<u>Can't Pay Attention and How to Think</u>

<u>Deeply Again</u>, by Johann Hari, he

interviewed neuroscientists and

sociologists who have studied focus for

many years and concluded that the
problem is both individual and
systemic. In one study, the average
American college student switches tasks
every 65 seconds while the median
amount of time they spend focusing on
one thing is 19 seconds. In another
study, researchers proved that adult
office workers spend only 3 minutes
focusing on a task, however, if they are
interrupted, it will take 23 minutes for
the worker to get back to that same state
of focus. If you add it all up, most
workers never get an hour of

uninterrupted focus in a day. Johann Hari identifies numerous causes for our loss of focus, but I readily identified two of the causes he identified. One, the technology you use today is designed to keep your attention because the more they can capture your attention, the more money they can make from advertisers. It's a business model that would require a systemic change for an entire industry and I see very little chance of a business making such a voluntary change without being forced by government intervention. Two, you need to be willing to say no. Say no to picking up your phone every 5 minutes to see if you have any new notifications; turn your notifications off. Say no to responding to every weekend email immediately just to show that you are part of the team. Say no to responding like a lab rat to every stimulus in your environment. Until you are willing to say no, you will always delay saying yes to what you want. When a painter paints or a writer writes, they have to say no to a lot of other stimuli. It's ok to get off the information rat wheel and take time away to focus. It's ok for other parts of your business or your life to go unattended for a while. When you are present, be present. I once took a trip with my boss in which we would be in a car for a 4-hour trip to meet with a supplier. I was excited because it was a fantastic opportunity for us to talk and get to know one another as he was new to the department. I volunteered to drive, so my boss jumped in the passenger seat and started checking his phone. For two hours on the way to our destination he responded to emails, texts, or took phone calls and then for two hours on the way back he did the same. As we pulled into the parking lot to end the trip, he looked up at me and said he should have sat in the back seat. What a lost opportunity. From that day forward, whenever I would take a road trip with one of my direct reports, I made it a point to use that time to get to know them and to give them a little insight into me. I found my relationships with those individuals were richer and more collegial after the trips.

Question 3: What are the Forces that enable Success?

When evaluating a client's vision for their success, I break that vision down into the three forces that will enable that success. The three forces are energy, motivation, and the environment. These forces are also the forces that an aviator must manipulate to successfully takeoff, fly, and land an airplane. Just like an aviator, you need to always begin with a plan.

During my military career I was a proud member of Air Force Special Operations where I got the opportunity to work with a lot of extremely high performing individuals such as Navy Seals and Army Green Berets. It was not what most people conjure up in their minds or what Hollywood portrays on television and in the movies. Everyone, regardless of rank, was expected to be the subject-matter expert in their specialty based on either being extremely knowledgeable and/or having a lot of experience. It was a small team environment where everyone would build their part of the plan in incredible detail with options based on multiple what-ifs. I always felt that by the time we got to the flight phase, the plan was so ingrained in our minds with all the options, that it made us very confident in our actions and each other's decision-making. We always planned for multiple contingencies because like life, things would inevitably not go as planned. Regardless, I believe that our planning sessions made dealing with the inevitable unplanned event easier because in our minds, we already understood our decision tree. This reduced decision times which in aviation can be the difference between life and death.

Once you have a vision of your success, the next step is to begin breaking your vision down into actionable goals to develop your plan. The goals that you develop need to be **S**pecific, **M**easurable, **A**ttainable, **R**elevant, and **T**ime-based or SMART goals. For example, at the end of the first year, law students can compete to become a

member of the coveted Law Review.
This is a specific goal because the
qualifications and requirements to
become a member of the Law Review
are clearly published for all students. It
is measurable because the result is either
yes or no. It can be attainable based on
their performance on the 10-day write-
on competition. It is relevant to the goal
of becoming a lawyer because it furthers
the student's knowledge of the law in a
perfunctory way. Finally, because
everything occurs in the 10-days after
the end of the spring semester, it is time-

bound.

S	**Specific** Clearly State your Goal
M	**Measurable** Ensure you can Measure Success
A	**Attainable** Set Goals you know you can Achieve
R	**Relevant** Set Goals Relevant to your Career or Education
T	**Time-Based** Set a Deadline for Completion

After identifying your SMART Goal, the next step is to break it down into realistic targeted actions. For example, your goal for days one through three may be to spend five hours each day researching and identifying the relevant case law for the write-on case. After each 5-hour period, you may want to reward yourself with something that rejuvenates your spirits, like doing yoga, long nature walks, or high intensity workouts. These small successes and their rewards will give you the motivation and confidence to keep pushing forward. Your next success may be having a rough draft completed by day four, again with an appropriate rejuvenating reward for yourself. This methodology of successive small successes with rejuvenating rewards would continue until announcement day. Regardless of whether you are successful in your goal, the process is the ultimate reward because it puts you in a growth mindset. You can be proud that you developed a plan, executed that plan, and if needed, you can adjust that plan for the next time. If you really want to live in a growth mindset, you can query those that were successful to understand how their process was different, so you can consider incorporating some of their process differences into your next SMART goal. Thus, the beauty of a growth mindset, you lose fear of rejection or failure when you focus on the process and getting better at your craft.

Part 1 Key Takeaways

You must continually define success for yourself at each phase of your life.

There are three dimensions to Your Success:

Health

Relationships

Career/Business

Success is achieved by breaking your Big Hairy Audacious Goals (BHAG) down into bite-size pieces.

Success begins with a Plan and SMART Goals
3 Forces enable Success:

Energy

Motivation

Environment

PART II: The Basics of Aviation

In this part, I will introduce and explain some terms used in aviation that form the foundation of my analogy between flying an airplane and running a business or leading a team. Over the course of my career, I have seen many similarities between organizational leadership and the process of flying an airplane. I see solopreneurs as fighter jet pilots because they are one-person operations charged with doing everything themselves. The level of inputs and stimulus can be overwhelming, so they must become masters of prioritization. Business leaders with less than 10 employees are more like leer jet pilots; there can be more than one in the flight station, but they are only responsible for a limited number of people due to the size of their aircraft. As small businesses grow into large corporations, they require an aircrew with specialized talents to achieve their multi-faceted missions and they are responsible for many more lives. Corporations are commensurate with commercial aviation. The Chief Executive Officer (CEO) is the pilot and ultimate decision-maker over where the airplane is headed, and the pilot is aided by the co-pilot or Chief Operating Officer (COO) who can take control and fly the plane/company as needed. The flight attendants or executive team are responsible for making sure all employees' needs are met so they are ready to tackle their daily duties. Regardless of the organization's size, effectively leading an organization requires the mastery of a skillset that is akin to flying an airplane. Understanding and identifying the forces that are impacting your planned route, a.k.a., exhibiting situational awareness, and quickly reacting to maneuver your organization through those forces to reach your objective is what every successful leader accomplishes time and time again. Microsoft, in my opinion, is a company that exemplifies this ability. I remember uploading MS-DOS software via disc and being amazed when Windows 95 came out with Internet Explorer. Now Microsoft has transitioned to being mostly cloud-based as the internet has developed over time and is a leader in investing in artificial intelligence. This is a company that recognizes the forces that are applying pressure, and they are adept at adjusting to maneuver the organization into a position to withstand those forces or move into completely new environments.

Chapter One: The Three Prioritized Actions of Aviators

In all instances aviators survive moment to moment by adhering to these three priorities of action: Aviate, Navigate, Communicate. To put it simply, their priority in all situations is to keep the airplane flying and their second priority is to make sure the airplane is headed in the right, unobstructed direction. After these two priorities are met, aviators then communicate with others to announce their intentions, provide notification of the modification of their course, or seek further assistance. However, every flight begins with a flight plan to enable deconfliction and promote safety of the airways. Flight planning entails determining the route, checking the weather forecasts along that route, and for some military aviators during combat operations, determining the threats along the route. For combat flights, once the initial plan is developed, more intensive combat planning involves counteracting each potential obstacle. For example, if a surface to air missile site is located right off the coast, an aircraft may fly exceedingly low, just skimming the ocean while getting spray mist on the windscreen, to avoid detection until it is too late for the surface to air missile site to react. I have found in my personal life that the times where I have been the most successful always began with a plan. I would get singularly focused, work on the bite-size plan, and then adjust quickly when things did not go as anticipated. The key to success in any situation is having enough situational awareness to know when the plan is unraveling and adjusting your approach quickly. In my first corporate job after military service, I worked for E&J Gallo Winery (Gallo) which at the time was either the largest winery in the United States of America or a very close second. Gallo was a very well-run organization; therefore, it was the leadership engine for the wine industry. Most Gallo alumni became executives in companies that either were direct competitors or serviced the wine industry in one way or another. The key rule at Gallo was to keep the company producing at all costs because the loss of shelf space in a store was akin to losing face in the Japanese culture, i.e., aviate. I started in Strategic Planning where we developed long-range and short-range plans to manage the wine supply, i.e., navigate. Finally, Gallo continues to be known for their ability to create and market the story behind their wines, i.e., communicate. For those of a certain age group, we all remember the folksy television commercials for Bartles and Jaymes, a

Gallo product, in the late 1980s. Now, let's dissect the relevance of each of these prioritized actions.

Aviate. The word aviate simply means to pilot or fly an airplane. Pilots are constantly monitoring the current situation, the forces acting on the aircraft, and taking appropriate countermeasures to maintain equilibrium or directing those forces in flight. Organizational leaders do the same thing, just exchange the word business for aircraft. When you aviate, you do not let the events around you interfere with your ability to focus on keeping the plane aloft or the business from failing. For example, one confidence maneuver that is taught in flight training is the nose-high stall. It involves pulling the nose of the aircraft up, like you are starting a climb to a higher altitude, but without increasing the power to sustain that climb. In a single engine Cessna, the plane starts to shutter just before entering the stall condition. Once the pilot feels the shutter, they are taught to lower the nose toward the ground to regain air speed, the life blood of an aircraft, so the

pilot can regain control of the aircraft for

further flight.

Figure A. Nose-High Stall

You can execute a nose-high stall by

attempting to take your business to

higher levels without the requisite

energy or power to sustain the climb. In

that case, you will usually experience

burnout and either cut back on your

plans or face potential loss of your business. You then need to lower the nose to build more energy reserves before attempting the maneuver again. You aviate in your life as well. If you are walking at night in an area known for crime, you are constantly surveying your surroundings for fight or flight cues. The hairs on your neck may start to stand up as you "feel" someone approaching you from behind or you may clinch the pepper spray in your purse as you see a potential threat approaching. These are real life examples of situational awareness and how you instinctively react. Pilots, however, understand the principles of aerodynamics so their reactions are based on their knowledge of how to manipulate the forces impacting their flight. You can also develop your understanding of forces and countermeasures so that your actions are steeped in deeper, unconscious brain, learning. Using my earlier example, someone who has years of martial arts training would know how to react if someone grabbed them from behind so they would be better prepared to fight.

This reminds me of a story that Jeff Blum, a family law attorney, shared with me. He had a female client who was very bright and very successful and the person she was divorcing was as well. She was almost ready to give up fighting for custody of her child because things were getting very nasty. Jeff, now retired, was a great family law attorney because he was always willing to be authentic with his clients and share his own experience with divorce. He was able to convince that client to stay in the battle and things eventually worked out well for her. She almost lost focus on what was truly important and fortunately for her, she had Jeff there to be that reminder. It was Jeff's experience that instinctively told him that if she continued without giving up, things could go her way. Never stop aviating.

Navigate. In larger aircraft specialized aircrew like navigators get the distinct honor of telling pilots where to go (pun intended). Navigators determine the aircraft's current location and provide course corrections, so situational awareness is as vital in navigating as it is in piloting. You must know where you are and where you want to go to plot a course to get there. Once on that course, you must constantly reassess your current position, identify the current and future forces that may take you off course, and adjust accordingly. Navigators, like business coaches, are constantly accounting for drift correction.

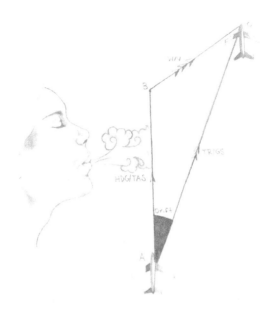

Figure B. Drift Correction

Using Figure B above for reference, a

pilot can set a heading (HDG) and a true

airspeed (TAS) to go from Point A to B,

but due to wind and the environment,

the plane may fly an actual ground track

(TR) and groundspeed (GS) to end up at

Point C due to drift. Navigators account for the current wind speeds and direction to adjust the heading and speeds that a pilot will fly so they arrive at their preferred destination, point B, both on time and on target.

Business owners and organizational leaders must constantly course correct their companies as well to account for external forces. It becomes extremely hard for organizations to reach their goals if environmental forces are impeding their progress and it is especially difficult if their leaders are

not situationally aware of those forces.
Have you ever heard the following?
Since it is impossible to predict the
future, a plan is worthless the moment it
is published. I, myself, have used this
logic to discount my reliance on
forecasting. But it is important to
distinguish between long-term and
short-term planning. If you are asked to
predict what you want for dinner each
day over the next six months, you
would be hard pressed to provide a
forecast that you could stick to without
changes. However, if you are asked

what you want for dinner over the course of the next two days, you could give you a reliable plan that you would more than likely follow. To me, this is the power of planning for the short term because it gives you much more flexibility to course correct as your tastes change or something influences you to make a different choice. Also, the iterative nature of short-term planning leads to more accurate results. Have you ever watched a cooking show and then had to change your meal plans because you wanted to try what you saw? Then you intuitively understand the power of short-term plans. Short-term planning is very useful in informing your long-term plan as well. When you notice and analyze how your short-term plans change, you can then project these changes onto your long-term plan. For example, if you notice in your short-term plans, you prefer mostly vegetarian meals, then you may forgo the purchase of half a cow from a butcher because you will not eat enough beef to justify the cost of the purchase. But...if it is impossible to predict the future, why not just take each day as it comes without a plan? Planning prepares your brain and your body to react appropriately. If you are cutting down a tree near your home, you would plan to cut down that tree so the probability of it hitting your home is exceptionally low. If you plan correctly, you will employ tie-offs and other methods to make the probability of it hitting your home virtually zero. The other option is to just start cutting and letting the tree fall where it may. In your opinion, which method has the greater likelihood of success? As for me, I highly recommend that you endeavor to always navigate.

Communicate. Once an aviator identifies their current situation and has plotted their course correction, they are free to communicate their intentions. For large airliners, communication is key to making sure they do not fly into other nearby aircraft. For example, if you are leaving your planned course to go around a thunderstorm, you must coordinate your deviation with flight control so they can ensure you do not encroach on another aircraft's path or potentially cause a mid-air collision. This is another good reason for every flight to file a flight plan with the appropriate authorities before taking off. To me, the rules of flying are like driving a car. You assume the other driver will stay in their lane because the rules give you predictability and safety. The same is true in your life and your organization. Whenever you make a change, it is important to let others know so they can help you or at a minimum do not get in the way of your progress. At best, others will support you in your new course.

Regardless of the size of your company, organizational leaders must be especially proficient in communicating their intentions. To be successful, organizational leaders must constantly be communicating with employees, stakeholders, constituents, and the community. Not just for deconfliction purposes, but also to inspire, motivate, and correct. This last part of the trifecta, communication, for organizational leaders is what drives organizational growth and evolvement, without which organizations cease to exist. Do not forget to communicate early and often. A good rule of thumb is that when you get tired of saying the same thing repeatedly, that's when most people start to listen.

Chapter Two: The Five Forces of Flight

In the study of aerodynamics, you learn to understand the properties of moving air and the interaction of solid bodies as they move through that air. These same properties and interactions are at play in our lives. There are forces that Lift us up, Drag that slows us down, energy that Thrusts us forward, and Weight that holds us down. When these forces are in balance, you experience stability, and it can seem as if you are on cruise control, just like an airplane at cruising altitude. When Thrust is greater than Drag, the aircraft moves forward and so do you. When Lift is greater than Weight and Drag, the aircraft can climb to higher altitudes and so can you. When the environment is stable, these forces can interact seamlessly but when there is turbulence, the environment can overwhelm the predictability with how these forces interact. The environment can throw all these forces out of whack so that it becomes impossible to keep an aircraft airborne or a business operating through no fault of the pilot/you.

The Five Basic Forces of Flight

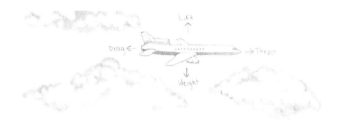

Figure C. The Five Basic Forces Acting on an Aircraft in Flight.

Thrust. The Thrust of an aircraft is a function of its engine(s) which accelerates the aircraft forward to achieve flight. More importantly, the amount of Thrust available is synonymous with the amount of potential energy. If you have no potential energy, then you cannot climb to a higher altitude.

If you have ever flown on a commercial airliner and sat near the wing, then you have experienced the following: when the pilots complete their climb to cruising altitude, the engines reduce their output, and you hear and feel less noise and vibration. At this point, the pilots are trading the kinetic energy needed for takeoff and climbing with potential energy to maximize endurance and range of the aircraft in flight. This tradeoff is important because when an aircraft reduces its Thrust to the minimum power required for its cruising airspeed, the pilots are ensuring they can reach their destination without running out of fuel. You should do the same thing in your life. Think about the times when you were looking for a new job, starting your own business, or taking an important exam that would enable you to improve your station in life. The excitement, the energy to work crazy long hours are all indicative of the Thrust (kinetic energy) needed to put you in a trajectory to achieve your goal(s). Thrust is important, but you cannot live on Thrust for exceedingly long periods of time because you will flame/burn out. That is why in your quest to improve your station in life, you need to reduce the Thrusters and cruise for a while to store up your potential energy to prepare for each successive climb. The same goes for organizational improvements. A lot of startups set their Thrust to 100% and thereby burnout just after takeoff both figuratively and literally. Business owners and organizational leaders must monitor their companies constantly for signs and symptoms of burnout, but more importantly, delay the start of new initiatives until stabilization of the current state so as not to burnout their people. A basic tenet of change management is to never give a team more than they can digest or comprehend at a given time, else you paralyze their forward progress.

Lissa Kreisler was inducted into the San Francisco Bay Area Radio Hall of Fame after 40 years in morning talk radio. She arrived at work by 3 am every day to prepare for her show that started at 5 am. Lissa always had a male partner, and she was designated as the "energy" (she did the color commentary), and he was the straight man. It didn't matter what was going on in her personal life, as soon as that microphone went on, she was performing. Every story she told, every newscast, she pretended like she was talking to one person, her best friend. Lissa's energy comes from treating everyone she meets as her best friend, and it is contagious. You cannot be around her without her energy infecting you as well. No one can fake that kind of energy for 40 years. According to Lissa, "My motivation was to make people feel good about themselves and to be happy. I didn't want to be that extra problem, I wanted them to be smiling. I never had a bad day because I never took myself so seriously."

Drag. Drag is the force that resists the aircraft from moving forward through the atmosphere and slows down forward progress. There are two types of Drag that can affect an aircraft's movement through the air. Induced Drag which comes from the production of Lift and is a function of the changing center of pressure of an aircraft as it moves through the atmosphere. As Lift increases, Drag also increases, thus increasing the requirement for more Thrust to climb. Another type of Drag is parasitic Drag. Parasitic Drag comes from all other sources such as the shape of the aircraft or wing and the texture of its surface, thus it is inherent in the systems' design.

You encounter induced Drag when you

need to overcome barriers to your success such as the scattered demands on your time that keep you from focusing. Your situational awareness can help recognize the existence of induced Drag because you can identify and feel the pressures blocking you from attaining your goals. An example of induced Drag in organizations is the inbox of each person's email account. Every day, organizations spend hours sifting through and responding to emails that are merely meant to inform others. Invariably each person replies to all so everyone can check them off as being informed or to add their two cents which do not alter the course of events in the original email. These replies fill the inboxes of multiple colleagues and organizational leaders for no reason other than allowing people to talk about their work. Feel free to quote me on this, in large organizations, most people spend as much or more time talking about their work as actually doing it. Very few issues get solved with an email exchange and an inbox with over 200 emails is a Drag on the energy of the inbox owner.

Parasitic Drag may not be overt in nature because it is inherent in the design. For example, a black female at the helm of a Fortune 500 company is rare, but not impossible. I am quite confident that Ursula Burns, the first black woman CEO to head a Fortune 500 company, had to overcome considerable parasitic Drag in her rise to the top. Parasitic Drag is often found in the form of organizational structures and norms that reward organizational talents unevenly. For example, an engineering firm assumes the CEO must be someone with an engineering background, when, the company can be run just as effectively with someone who has a background in business. Therefore, parasitic Drag is often not recognizable or apparent, but it does exist.

Lift. Lift is the force on an aircraft that enables it to takeoff, climb, maintain level flight, and land. For a plane to takeoff, climb, or land, Lift must be greater than Drag and Weight. Lift acts through an aircraft's center of pressure and the distribution of Lift forces about

an aircraft contributes to its control and

stability. As Thrust increases the airflow

over the surface of the wing, due to the

shape of the wing, there is greater force

on the bottom surface than on the top

which results in increasing Lift.

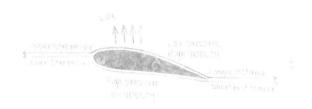

Figure D. Lift

Lift is the force that gives rise to your

altitude and your success. Most people

associate their station in life or altitude to their financial status or net worth, however, I also include a state of happiness and peace of mind when I consider a person's station in life. Peace of mind is worth more than two lifetimes of gold and silver. Lift is what takes us to that higher altitude in life, however we choose to define it. For organizations, Lift is synonymous with growth. Very few business owners start out in business with the desire to limit the growth of their companies. Most want to see how large their businesses can grow or how high their organizations can climb.

Weight. In level flight, Weight equals Lift. While Weight is evenly distributed throughout an aircraft, we often think of it as rotating about the center of gravity. During flight, an aircraft's Weight constantly changes due to fuel consumption, so the center of gravity is also changing. If the Weight is greater than Lift, the aircraft will not fly which is why during some emergencies after takeoff, pilots must dump fuel to get to an aircraft's landing Weight.

Organizations must do the same sometimes during an emergency. Larger corporations shudder businesses quickly and layoff thousands of employees in reaction to short term economic situations.

Weight is the counter force to Lift. It holds us back in our lives from achieving the altitudes that we desire. For example, an addict must overcome the Weight of addiction if they desire stability or peace in their life. We all have burdens to bear, but if we can maintain our situational awareness to keep those burdens at bay, we can generate more Lift to keep us aloft thus moving higher toward our goals.

The Atmosphere/Environment. The environment in which we operate impacts us more than we may realize. Worse yet, it is a force upon which we have little or no control. For an aircraft, the atmosphere changes from place to place, day to day, and minute to minute, because it is a complex mixture of water vapor and gases. Most aircraft operate in the troposphere which extends from the earth's surface to about 35,000 feet and is characterized by turbulent conditions where large changes in temperature and humidity are common.

Directly above the troposphere is the tropopause which is a transition layer leading into the stratosphere. The stratosphere is characterized by level temperatures and greater stability. The exact altitude of these atmospheres' changes with the barometric pressure of a location. For example, the barometric pressure in Dallas, Texas is different from the barometric pressure in Seattle, Washington. Most commercial airliners cruise at altitudes between 35,000 and 39,000 feet on longer flights which are the lower levels of the stratosphere.

Normally, at these altitudes there is less turbulence with higher winds which can dramatically impact both fuel consumption and length of time in flight. When an airplane has a large tailwind, they do not require as much Thrust to achieve higher airspeeds which results in a shorter flight and less fuel consumption. Tailwinds are why you may land 20 minutes early when flying from the west coast to the east coast. There is an inverse relationship with headwinds; the aircraft will require more Thrust to achieve an airspeed, thus resulting in more fuel consumption and a longer flight time.

Both our lives and organizations are impacted by headwinds and tailwinds like an airplane.

Some people are born on third base and go through life thinking they hit a triple.

~ Barry Switzer

I think Barry Switzer's quote is emblematic of how some are born into more fortunate circumstances or environments and have a tailwind at their backs, whether they realize it or not. Others are born with every headwind imaginable, yet they still manage to succeed in life. How do they do it? They develop exceptional situational awareness skills, and they act on what they are sensing from their environment. The same is true for organizations and organizational leaders. Organizations that make situational awareness a core value can be more successful in the long-term because they can adjust to changing market conditions more rapidly. When the Covid-19 pandemic began in early 2020, restaurants were hit especially hard because most relied on indoor, sit-down dining. The survivors not only adjusted to takeout dining, but they also made takeout dining more convenient with curbside pickup and the use of delivery apps. As outdoor dining became an option, they quickly erected tents or road barriers so diners could enjoy the sit-down dining experience again while outside. Those that could not adjust their model, really suffered and most are no longer in business. Another plug for built-in short-term planning and flexibility.

Aviators use atmospheric pressure to determine their airspeed, altitude, and to help them increase the force of Lift on an aircraft. In addition, air density can impact the length of runway cargo aircraft need for takeoff, and what payload capacity they can carry. This atmospheric pressure decreases as altitude increases, as you move from the troposphere to the stratosphere. Thus, I surmise that the higher you can rise in life, the less impact the environment has on you. The financial crisis of 2008 is a prime example of this last statement. "Too big to fail" was the justification for the federal government bailing out large banks over smaller banks. The reason being that large banks are so interconnected that if they failed, there would be further reverberations in the economy that would contribute to the collapse of several world economies. Thus, while other smaller banks failed and the economy faltered, the too big to fail banks never left the stable environs of their stratosphere.

Chapter 1 and 2 Key

Takeaways

Aviators survive by committing to the following priorities: (1) Aviate, (2) Navigate, (3) Communicate.

There are five forces in the study of aerodynamics that impact an aircraft: (1) Thrust, (2) Drag, (3) Lift, (4) Weight, and (5) Environment/Atmosphere.

Thrust accelerates the aircraft forward and is required to produce Lift.

Kinetic energy is energy in use.

Potential energy is energy not in use, yet available.

Drag is a counterforce to Thrust thereby slowing down an aircraft's forward progress.

Induced Drag is visible and recognizable.

Parasitic Drag is a function of the design of the system.

Lift is the force that causes an aircraft to fly.

To takeoff, the Lift force must be greater than Drag and Weight.

Weight is the counterforce to Lift and is the only predictable force impacting an aircraft.

The environment has a definite impact on an aircraft's ability to fly, however, we can overcome most environmental factors with planning and situational awareness.

In the next chapter we will identify and

discuss the 3 key elements of

organizational success.

Chapter Three: The 3 Key Elements of Success

The four forces that enable an airplane to move through the air are the same forces that enable or hinder you from achieving success. While Thrust and Drag are two opposing forms of energy; Lift and Weight are two opposing forms of motivation. Finally, none of these forces can propel a business toward success without a supportive environment. Therefore, the 3 key elements of business success are energy, motivation, and a supportive environment. Just as an aircraft must first move forward by Thrust before it can Lift off for flight, the expenditure of energy also comes before the motivation to improve or climb higher. You cannot motivate your way off the couch because motivation is a by-product of energy expenditure. Interestingly, it takes the expenditure of energy, i.e., action to motivate you. Therefore, the prime imperative is a bias toward action. Motivation is about improving your current circumstances. When I first started barbecuing for my family, I was horrible at it. The meat was under-cooked, and the vegetables were never quite right. I could have just given up, but something clicked inside of me. I remembered that my grandmother always said that her cooking was so good because she put all her love into it. So, I was motivated to show my love for my family by becoming a better cook. Voila, years later, they each have a dish or a meal that is their favorite that I enjoy cooking for them because, like my grandmother, it is how I express my love. So, I had to expend the energy to start cooking and barbecuing so I could learn how bad I was at it which motivated me to get better so I could express my love for my family through this medium.

Energy

Every journey begins with an expenditure of energy. When our bodies are not healthy enough to generate the needed kinetic energy for movement, little forward progress is possible. For example, a cancer patient who is getting chemotherapy treatments would not likely be able to produce enough kinetic energy to run a marathon. Even as you are cruising through life, you need a store of potential energy as it is essential to your overall health. A good night's sleep restores your energy reserves which gives you the power to aviate and navigate your company. The interplay of kinetic and potential energy is instrumental in whether you achieve your business goals. Regardless of what you want to accomplish in life, it will take energy to do it. Therefore, just like in an airplane, energy management is key to leadership and to your journey.

Have you ever been so immersed in what you were doing that you did not realize how much time had passed? This sweet spot of energy consumption is commonly referred to as being in the zone, a.k.a., cruise control. Humans perform at their best while in the zone which is why it is the goal of every athlete to play in the zone as often and as long as possible. However, being in the zone does not only apply to athletes. The factory floor worker who is so enmeshed in their routine that they do not even realize it is end of day and then they leave wondering where the day went performs in the zone as well. Depending on the efficiency of the process, the same factory floor worker is not tired at the end of the day. The activity is not relevant, because zone performance is almost effortless to the human mind, just like a plane at cruising altitude in a stable atmosphere. You do not fully experience any surrounding turbulence while in the zone, even though it may be all around you, because you are so focused on the task at hand.

Businesses can operate in the zone as well. It usually happens when an overwhelming majority of team members are pulling on the same side of the rope and in unison. It is especially infectious when a business is experiencing growth and success. The adage that success feeds more success is also indicative of a business that is performing in the zone for a long period of time.

When we talk about Thrust in the context of human behavior, it gets us off the couch and sustains us as we accomplish our goals. Therefore, when analyzing your current reality, you need to identify from where your energy comes. What gives you energy? How can you do more of that gives you energy? The storing of potential energy for later use must be a key priority in your life. If sleep is what gives you the energy to face the day, then sleep must be a top priority and you must treat it as such. For some people, it is exercise and for others it may be taking a vacation, so energy rejuvenation is unique to each individual person. It is also important that we identify what rejuvenates others as well, especially our life partners, and ensure they get the time they require to replenish their energy stores.

What keeps us from moving forward with our lives? Drag. I hear it all the time, I am too busy surviving my day-to-day life to even think of developing 90-day goals for my business. I would like to reframe this to the following question: are you prepared to spend the rest of your life just surviving the day to day or would you rather be thriving? The biggest culprit of induced Drag is the "busyness" of life. Somehow, many have bought into the lie that being busy is being productive. We all like getting things done, but the happiest and most well-adjusted people get the right things done; the most effective things done. In a lot of respects, the people who are too busy to develop 90-day goals are the same people who would benefit the most from taking the time to develop them.

In my coaching, I find many people get efficiency and effectiveness confused. Efficiency focuses on getting things done timely with the least amount of effort. However, effectiveness focuses on getting the right things done, thereby reducing wasted effort. The following story depicts the difference between these two: While I was still on active duty in the Air Force, my unit received a short notice request from a special operations team stationed in another country for transport to an undisclosed location. When we arrived to pick them up, they wanted to load a wide variety of their equipment on board but as the loadmaster evaluated the Weight, he quickly determined they would have to leave some of it behind. This situation was neither efficient nor effective at this point. I was then charged with writing the standard operating procedures with all nearby special operations teams so this would not happen again. So, I spent time with our Army and Navy brethren to capture their mission types and equipment requirements so our loadmasters could develop standard load plans and configurations for them. This way, when we showed up, they would have the equipment staged for a quick load. Our focus was not only on efficiency. Because these documents also shared knowledge of how each unit operates, the terms used and their meanings, and how each is organized, it became an effective means for our organizations to communicate and understand each other. It just so happens that 20 years after I wrote those documents, one of my Air Force Academy classmates became the commander of my old unit and he told me that they still use those documents, although I am sure they have been updated and revised numerous times in the spirit of continuous improvement. Parasitic Drag is not as obvious to spot because it is built into the design of the business. It hides in the shadows and is foisted upon us without our knowing and it is often too late when we do recognize its effects. Parasitic Drag slows down your progress and makes you expend more energy than is needed, just like when an aircraft experiences a strong headwind. Therefore, you need to be on the lookout for it by noticing events or times where it takes more energy than needed to reach your goals. Take a toxic organizational culture for example. A company that experiences many people leaving and simply re-organizes the workload for those left behind is creating their own parasitic Drag. Those who are left behind with more work can become overwhelmed, less effective, and less efficient over time, especially if changes to the core process of how they do their work do not change. If the mass exodus continues, this parasitic Drag can become debilitating to the proper functioning of the company.

Motivation

Lift is the force that takes us to higher levels of success, and it is driven by our motivation. Motivation is what encourages us and our organizations to expend the energy to overcome Drag to create Lift. The question is simply; what motivates you to want to change your current circumstances? Once that motivation is identified, and energy is expended, Lift can occur. Without the proper motivation, however, Lift will not occur. For example, most businesses that are started with the primary purpose of making a quick buck for the owner do not last for generations. As EBAY was first taking off in the 1990s, many people quit their jobs to sell their "stuff" on the internet. Many of these businesses did not survive the onslaught of negative customer reviews when their goods did not arrive on time or were damaged in transit. The EBAY seller had no real control over these occurrences but that did not matter. However, those businesses that are motivated and focused to fulfill a specific need or a want of their customers, have a higher chance of becoming a multi-generational company. A great example of this is Amazon which started as an online bookstore. They fulfilled a specific need for their customers and in building a more reliable supply chain, they were able to pivot into various other sources of revenue, such as a wide variety of consumer goods and video streaming. You see, if your organization does not produce value for others, more than likely, you will not be able to maintain your current altitude or climb to new heights.

Whatever does not Lift us up, weighs us down. Every person you meet has experienced turbulence in their life, absolutely no one is immune. What differs is the severity of the turbulence. The turbulence you have experienced in your life is what underlies your internal doubts and fears. Thus, with proper motivation, you can put aside those doubts and fears to expend the energy required to produce Lift.

The reason you need to identify

the Lift and Weight affecting your life is that they each give us clarity into what is motivating us to expend the energy needed to drive change. Without the appropriate motivation, nothing worth doing gets done. Martin Fishman, MD, MPA is the president of a large ophthalmology medical-surgical group, Spectrum Eye Physicians, Inc., based in Northern California. He also is a director in "Seeing Again Guatemala", a volunteer organization that has provided medical and surgical eye care and surgery to a poor indigenous population in the highlands of Guatemala since 1996. The program works at a medical clinic that was first started in 1964 by the Diocese of Helena, Montana, after Pope Paul VI encouraged Catholics in wealthy countries to provide aid to poorer communities in need throughout the world. The Clinica Maxena was built by the Diocese in Santo Thomas la Union, Suchitepequez, Guatemala, a town of 7,000 people, in the Guatemalan highlands. It now serves an area of over 70,000 throughout the year with a full time Guatemalan general physician. In 1996, an ophthalmologist from Santa Cruz, CA, who was also a Rotarian, began to work with volunteers to provide eye care and surgery at the Clinica. Since then, two groups of volunteers, including ophthalmologic surgeons and operating room staff, travel twice a year to the clinic. Each mission trip provides medical eye care to over 300 patients, and about 50-60 people who are totally blind from cataracts undergo operations, with their vision restored the next day. All this good came from a

simple inspiring thought from the Pope,
a commitment to another part of the
world by the Diocese of Helena, and the
work of volunteers from all over the
United States of America.

Environment

When it comes to assessing the
environment in which you operate, you
should think in terms of turbulence. If
you have ever been on an airplane that
experienced severe turbulence, you
understand how disruptive and
damaging it can be. Aviators avoid
turbulence not just because it is

uncomfortable, but turbulence can knock an airplane out of the sky by damaging it structurally. The same is true for humans. A toxic, turbulent environment damages you structurally and keeps you from achieving and maintaining flight.

Often when you are experiencing turbulent times, you can lose focus on your goals and revert to merely existing, merely getting by from day to day. It is precisely at these moments that you need to hang on to hope. Hope gives you the ability to dream of changing your altitude and your environment.

Without hope, you can become a victim

of your environment, directionless, and

without any Thrust to move forward

and create a Lift. Many large companies

that had high hopes for a quick rebound

from the Covid-19 pandemic in the

summer of 2021 due to the vaccine, are

now revising their plans to coexist with

Covid versus eradicating it. Let's face it,

the global pandemic has shown you the

power of your environment to shape

your life. I firmly believe those

companies that are adjusting their

strategies now so that future pandemics do not have as large an impact, are moving to become multi-generational companies. Automation, new modalities of moving goods, use of technology to allow knowledge workers to work from anywhere and even contactless payment are prime examples of innovation cycles that have been sped up in response to the environment. Unfortunately, these changes may have detrimental effects on many in our society who depend on jobs that cannot be done remotely.

Chapter 3 Key Takeaways

There are 3 key elements that impact organizational success: (1) Energy, (2) Motivation, and (3) Supportive Environment

Energy is a function of the forces of Thrust and Drag. It is the first element that must exist for success to occur.

Motivation is a function of the forces of Lift and Weight. Motivation is a byproduct of Energy.

A Supportive Environment is required for organizational success to occur.

In the next part, you will learn how to use and leverage your knowledge of the four basic forces to set your goals and develop a strategic plan to elevate your current altitude.

PART III: Knowledge in Action

Knowledge is useful when it can be used to help you in your life. In this part of the book, I will discuss how to apply the three forces to drive change and help you achieve your goals and aspirations.

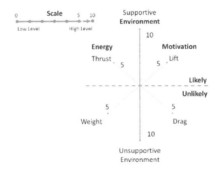

Success = f {Energy + Motivation + Environment}
Energy = Thrust – Drag
Motivation = Lift – Weight

Environment = Level of Supportiveness –
Level of Unsupportiveness
Likelihood of Success > 0, Likely
Likelihood of Success ≤ 0, Unlikely

Chapter Four: Assessing Your Current Situation

Understanding the three key elements for success and how they are currently impacting your journey are vital to establishing good situational awareness. In this chapter, I will guide you through how to identify the current forces as they impact your business results, your organization's culture, or your personal life. It is important that you assess each part independently and identify potential overlap. Once identified, you must face reality and develop plans to play to your strengths while managing or relying on your relationships to offset your weaknesses.

Energy

For an airplane to takeoff, there must be sufficient Thrust applied to generate the required amount of Lift. Therefore, you always begin your assessment by identifying the amount of Thrust you can generate because the amount of Thrust available is equivalent to your potential energy. Some activities build your potential energy while others deplete your energy. Therefore, Thrust is identified by answering the following questions:

- How do you rejuvenate? Are you feeling up for the challenge?

- What gives you energy to get through the day? When was the last time you regenerated your energy reserves?

- What makes you feel alive? When was the last time you did what makes you feel alive?

I was downsized during the pandemic, and I went through a short period where it was hard to generate any Thrust because I was lost. I knew that if I did not get up every morning and establish a routine, I could quickly spiral into a depression. So, my Thrust during this period came from building and following a routine that kept me busy but allowed time for me to really think through what to do next. After assessing my strengths, weaknesses, and what I enjoyed most about being in executive leadership, I realized that facilitating teams, along with coaching and mentoring people was the Thrust in my business life. It is what made my days go faster and provided me with the energy to push through the other responsibilities. Therefore, starting a coaching business was the best way for me to channel my energy.

Every positive force has a negative counter-acting force. Drag is what depletes your energy. When you look at Drag, you must look at it in two respects. Induced Drag includes all the things you do to yourself that holds you back. For example, overscheduling yourself to the point of burnout. Parasitic Drag includes those forces that hold you back but are not influenced by your actions. For example, an underlying characteristic over which you have little control such as an underlying trauma from childhood. Thus, the questions you ask yourself are as follows:

- What robs you of the energy needed to get through each day? Do I do it out of habit or for some other reason?

- What is slowing your progress? Is it something over which you can exercise control? Are you addicted to majoring in minor things?

- Are there avenues for getting help? Can you delegate or outsource it to others?

- Is this a short-term or long-term Drag on me and my goals?

Minimizing Drag in your life is imperative to achieving your goals. There will always be things that hold you back from moving forward, but they are not always bad things. A parent who takes parental leave to be with a newborn child may experience a short-term Drag on their career but an overall Thrust in their personal life for the long-term. Most important is that you identify your current Drag with an understanding of its total impact.

Motivation

Lift is a function of Thrust, Drag, and Weight. These three forces must be coordinated and controlled in a way that will enable the airplane to Lift off the ground, stay in flight, and land. In many respects, Lift is the driving force behind flight because without Lift, you cannot get or stay airborne. When determining your Lift, you should ask the following questions:

- Why do you want to improve or grow your business? What is your goal?

- Who or what is driving the need for change? Is it a make-or-break situation?

- Do you have enough potential energy or Thrust to sustain your quest for improvement or growth?

Lift, in many respects, is life sustaining because without the motivation to survive and thrive, you deteriorate. In all phases of growth, you need to seek to optimize the amount of Lift you can create regardless of what phase of the growth cycle you are in. Even when a plane is landing, it is generating Lift, else the plane would drop like a rock which would make for an uncomfortable and damage producing landing.

The counter force to Lift is Weight. You can be motivated to conquer the world but there will always be some opposite force that weighs in the back of your mind. Questions like, am I good enough will temper your motivations by weighing you down. When determining what is potentially weighing you down, you should ask the following questions:

- Am I operating from a fixed or a growth mindset?

- What negative thoughts are weighing on me? Where are these negative thoughts coming from?

- Is there anything from your past that may be holding you back? For example, post-traumatic stress. Where can you get help to deal with what is holding you back?

- What would you gain from presenting your best self to the world?

Weight is the one force that should be the easiest to identify because we are forced to deal with it from the beginning. It is also in the design of the organizational structure, like parasitic Drag, and is not as transitory as the other forces. When an aircraft takes off, the pilot knows how much it weighs and based on fuel consumption rates, can accurately predict what Weight the aircraft needs to be when landing. You can readily know what is weighing you down when you decide to climb to a higher altitude in your organization and can work over the course of the climb to reduce the effects of that Weight. For example, an organization that needs to raise capital to fund their growth will

know that prior to initiating a change

for growth.

Environment

The medium through which you

move, your environment, can have a

significant impact on your growth and

ability to climb higher in life. While it

can be an impediment, you can choose

to move into more hospitable

environments that are supportive of

your efforts. Movement from one

environment to another requires tough

choices that many people do not make

because they are fearful of change.

When accessing your environment, some key questions to ask yourself are:

- Does this environment support my attempts to achieve my goals? What would a supportive environment look like?

- Can I impact a change in my environment that could facilitate my growth? How long would it take for that change to take effect?

- Is there a considerable amount of turbulence and instability in this environment? How have others in the same environment handled the turbulence and instability?

Another component of your environment is the amount of noise that you must cut through to accomplish your goals. Technological advancements have made us more productive, but it has also made us overwhelmed with busyness. Information overload is common for us all but is especially poignant for knowledge workers. Environments that encourage the creation of more noise make it harder for you to break through to success. Organizations can do everything right. They can have the proper motivation and have enough energy to climb into the stratosphere but can still fail because they are operating in a non-supportive environment. A prime example is Blockbuster video. I once heard Marc Randolph, the co-founder of Netflix, tell the story of how he went to Blockbuster headquarters with his partner Reed Hastings to discuss Blockbuster buying Netflix. Blockbuster refused. As the internet exploded in the early 2000's, Blockbuster was caught flatfooted to the environmental change and by 2019, only one Blockbuster video store remained while Netflix continually adapted to the changing environment to become a major success. Just like an airplane maneuvering around a thunderstorm, Netflix continued to maneuver from online ordering of DVD rentals shipped to your home to kiosks in grocery stores to online streaming. The moral of the story is simple, organizations must be willing to change and move as the environment changes to find support for their growth. You must be willing to do the same.

Likelihood of Success (LoS) Model

The following model, Figure E, is used to assess your current situation to determine your likelihood of success when attempting to climb to a higher altitude.

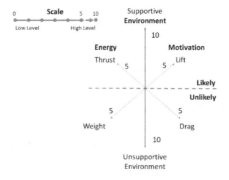

Figure E. The Likelihood of Success Model

LoS = Energy + Motivation + Environment
Energy = Thrust − Drag
Motivation = Lift − Weight
Environment = Supportive − Unsupportive
LoS > 0, Likely
LoS ≤ 0, Unlikely

The key to understanding the model is the scaling, which is skewed towards the environment. This is simply because regardless of your energy and motivation, without a supportive environment, success is much more difficult if not impossible. Just like the outsized impact the environment has on an airplane; environment plays an outsized part in your life and business as well.

Case Study. In the mid-1980s an optician, Haryl, takes a well-deserved vacation to New York from Boston after successfully expanding his business to three locations. While in New York this optician stumbles upon a new store called LensCrafters. This business owner has never seen an optician store with about 15 sales representatives to wait on customers, nor the volume and variety of different frame options. They had more options in that one location than he had in all three of his locations. This owner immediately asks, how can I possibly compete with this? After doing some research, he discovers that LensCrafters has the backing of a billion-dollar company, so expansion is only a matter of when, not if. Looking at these factors, the likelihood of success analysis follows:

Environment. For years, opticians operated on over 80% gross margins. With such high margins, it was only a matter of time before larger, well-funded companies disrupted the eyewear industry. In addition, LensCrafters offered the customer glasses in about an hour with a price match guarantee. Based on the speed, quality, and variety that LensCrafters offered its customers, I would rate the LoS in this environment a negative 5. Once this type of store opened in Boston, it would be very hard to compete with the glasses in about an hour guarantee. One of the locations that this business owner had just acquired was in Harvard Square, Cambridge Massachusetts. This was right in the heart of the many tourists who would come to visit Harvard

University and very convenient for students. Invariably tourists would forget to bring their sunglasses or accidentally break a pair of glasses during their travels. With less than 5 employees, there was no way for him to turnaround a new pair of prescription glasses in less than an hour. In addition, LensCrafters had such scale, that competing on price would drop margins so low that he would not be able to continue to grow his small business.

Energy. After much soul-searching, Haryl determined that he just did not have the energy to take on a direct threat as large and well-funded as LensCrafters. Using the LoS model, I would rate the amount of Thrust available to be a 4 but this Thrust is offset by a Drag rating of -4. Therefore, the overall energy rating is zero.

Motivation. With only 5 employees against thousands in the LensCrafters organization, I would give the amount of Lift available a low 2. It would take unparalleled rapid growth to be a serious competitor to LensCrafters but based on location and local covenants, there may have been a way to carve out a niche business with limited growth. This would mean a considerable Weight on the expansion opportunities so I would rate that negative 5 for an overall motivation score of negative 3.

Likelihood of Success. With Energy equal to zero, Motivation equal to negative 3, and Environment scoring a negative 5, the likelihood of success is a negative 8, or highly unlikely. Based on this likelihood of success, I would recommend to Haryl that he find other productive ways to spend his time. Fortunately, Haryl did just that and sold his optician business in the 1990s. Fast forward to 2015, Haryl went back to Boston and decided to visit his old Harvard Square location, the crowning jewel of his previous optical empire. Haryl walks into the store where he sees this young man who appears to own the store, so he asks him if he is the owner to which the man responds, yes, I own it with my father. So Haryl introduces himself and the man immediately recognizes his name and calls for his father. Turns out, his father was the son of the Optometrist who bought the 3 locations from Haryl. They talk for about 10 or 15 minutes and the current owner shares that internet-based optical companies like Warby Parker, Glasses USA, and Roka have squeezed margins for both the big box and smaller, independent retail stores. Fortunately, they were still open and surviving in this competitive environment, a testament to their grit.

Haryl's ability to effectively monitor his

environment is what made him successful in business. Regardless of whether selling when he did was the right thing to do, the most important point is that he was able to detect the landscape shifting underneath his feet, i.e., he was situationally aware. Knowing when to get out is just as important as knowing when to get in. Even while he clearly had the energy and the motivation to continue in the optical retail space, he got a glimpse into the future during his visit to New York and determined he did not want to participate in the race to the bottom of

lower margins.

Chapter 4 Key Takeaways

Energy

Thrust

How do you rejuvenate?

What gives you energy to get through the day?

What makes you feel alive?

Drag

What robs you of the energy needed to get through each day?

What is slowing your progress? Is it something over which you can exercise control?

Are there avenues for getting help?
If I address this issue, will I feel energized?

Motivation

Lift

> Why do you want to change your current altitude?

> Whom or what is encouraging the change? Is there enough Lift to sustain you at the newer altitude?

Weight

> What negative thoughts are weighing on you?

> Is there anything from your past that you need to manage that may be holding you down? For example, post-traumatic stress.

> What prevents you from presenting your best self to the world?

Environment

> Does this environment support my attempts to achieve my goals?

> Does this environment promote obstacles to the achievement of my goals?

> Is there a considerable amount of turbulence and instability in this environment?

Likelihood of Success Model

> Without a supportive environment, it is very difficult to achieve success.

> This model can also help an organization set priorities for major projects.

In the next chapter, you will learn how to use and maneuver these forces to achieve success.

Chapter Five: Maneuvering for Success

Knowing and understanding the forces at play are important but above all is understanding how to manipulate these forces to your advantage or for your survival. In this chapter I introduce the core phases of flight and how aviators manipulate these forces in each phase to achieve their objectives. Fortunately, these phases of flight correspond with many of the phases of a business. For example, landing an airplane is synonymous with a business owner retiring and transitioning their business to their children or a willing buyer.

Planning

Every flight begins with a flight plan. Our plans are merely physical manifestations of our vision, goals, and objectives. Normally, flight planning begins with an assessment of the environment, i.e., the weather. Therefore, organizations should begin their short-term planning with an assessment of their current environment. This environmental analysis should focus on building current situational awareness and should be done quarterly.

Just as in flying, all plans should be written so they can be referred to often to ensure the organization is heading toward its desired destination and that daily decisions are made with the plan in mind. It is important that companies do not get analysis paralysis when developing plans. The type of planning that I am advocating is quick, directional, and flexible because it is revised quarterly.

I was fortunate enough to meet with

Erik van der Burg, CEO, Co-founder of Venova Medical, Inc. Erik is a serial entrepreneur in the medical device industry with several of his inventions/companies being bought by larger medical device companies. In today's business world, ideas are vetted thoroughly before anyone will invest in companies outside of friends and family. To get a professional investor to put money in, like a Venture Capitalist, they want you to have the course from takeoff to landing all plotted out and a reasonable amount of certainty for each step of the way. According to Erik, 20 or 30 years ago when he started his entrepreneurial journey, if you had an idea and maybe a patent filed and a single big name saying your idea made sense, people would readily invest in your concept. Now you have to have your idea, you need to have data from studies conducted on appropriate human substitutes, you need to have bench top proof of manufacturing concept, maybe 5 key opinion leaders all saying what you're doing is good, you need to have the reimbursement pathway figured out, you need to have your regulatory pathway figured out and if any of those things look tough or questionable or uncertain, investors will likely not invest.

While a company's vision may include becoming the largest car manufacturer in the world, the only way to get there is to provide each customer with a quality vehicle that meets their wants and desires at a price they are willing to pay. Developing a vision is a vital part of the long-term planning process, but goal setting is the bedrock of short-term planning. The more consistent you are in identifying your short-term goals and working toward them, the more likely you are to achieve your long-term vision. Thus, short-term planning gives you direction, just like a navigator, and helps you realize when you are not being consistent and are off course steering away from your ultimate vision.

Takeoff

When an aviator gets clearance to takeoff, they use Thrust to push the airplane forward down the runway to reach their takeoff speed. At speed, the pilot vectors the Thrust upward to create Lift beneath the wings of the aircraft to achieve flight. The early stages of takeoff are monitored closely as the pilot retracts the landing gear to reduce Drag, thereby creating more Lift. Takeoff is all about overcoming Drag and Weight.

When a teenager or young adult leaves their home for the first time, they are executing a takeoff maneuver. Hopefully, they have an adult who is monitoring every stage of the takeoff and providing support and instruction, so they can achieve flight. It is important that they have enough Thrust to create enough Lift for takeoff. Failure to Lift off leaves a person or an organization without the ability to experience the positive feelings associated with the achievement of goals. Startups are delicate and the failure rate is high because there are so many dials and warning lights going off that it is hard to find and focus on the one switch that may keep the organization aloft. So many aircraft accidents happen because a pilot and/or crew forget to aviate first and get distracted by a light. It is even more perilous as a solopreneur because there is no one else there to break the focus on the distraction. Startups that have succeeded were able to navigate the distractions and stayed focused on building a reliable cash flow which enabled them to survive and sometimes thrive.

If someone has trouble taking off, the following questions and the answers to them can determine the best course(s) of action to take.

1. Do I have enough Thrust to move forward?

2. If I cannot generate enough Thrust, is it my inability to generate enough Lift? Can I get rid of the Drag, or Weight that is holding me back?

3. How can I generate more potential energy to convert to kinetic energy?

Climbing To Higher Altitude

Once the climb is established, the focus shifts to monitoring for burnout or the point where a person or organization runs out of kinetic energy. A sustained climb burns a lot of fuel in both an airplane and an organization. Just as in a plane, it is important to keep potential energy in reserve, i.e., do not set your engines to maximum throttle. Each time a designated altitude is reached, throttle back on the Thrust to achieve a cruising airspeed. In organizations, this gives your team time to make small adjustments and improvements to the current state. However, you never want to linger at one altitude for too long because complacency will set it and your organization will cease to grow. The same can be said for your life. As humans, we tend to take things and people for granted, especially when it comes to our relationships. Therefore, we need to refresh things from time to time by challenging ourselves to stimulate growth. Organizations and people who do not innovate or grow die. So leaders need to continue to push to higher altitudes. Therefore, leaders need to understand The Improvement Cycle and incorporate it into their change management plans. It is important for organizational health to provide a recovery and standardization phase in any improvement to give everyone a chance to internalize the change. Once they have done so, then the leader should move the organization into another improvement phase. The strategic plan must account for the time it will take to reach the goal.

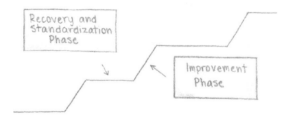

Figure F. The Improvement Cycle

Descending To Lower Altitude

From time to time, organizations and

people need to retrench, regroup, and simplify things. When descending to a lower altitude, you are building your potential energy stores in the descent for the next push. Gaining airspeed in the descent, just like after a nose-high stall, helps you gain back control of the aircraft and your organization. There is nothing wrong with taking your organization to a lower altitude for a time, especially after attempting a maneuver that could have resulted in a large increase in altitude. The important thing to remember is that you cannot stay at a lower altitude for too long else it can become too comfortable, thus impeding future growth.

Landing

Every airplane must land at some time, just as every business is either sold or transferred to the next generation. Landing an airplane is difficult because you must maintain enough Lift while descending to prevent crashing or landing extremely hard and damaging the aircraft. When an organizational leader is transferring ownership of the enterprise, they are essentially doing a touch and go landing of the organization. Once again, there needs to be enough Lift for the next owner to take control after the smooth landing and continue with a smooth takeoff under their leadership. The same goes for the end of a person's career. If you are fortunate enough to have reached retirement age, then a smooth transition is extremely important. So, landing an airplane, an organization, or a career is one of the most delicate maneuvers to accomplish as a leader.

Chapter 5 Key Takeaways

Organizational planning should begin with an assessment of the environment.

Short-term goal accomplishment is more likely when consistent actions are taken.

The following questions should be answered before an organization takes off:

> Do I have enough Thrust to move forward?

> If I cannot generate enough Thrust, is it my inability to generate enough Lift, too much Drag, or too much Weight that is holding me back?

> How can I generate more potential energy to convert to kinetic energy?

> How can I create more Lift or reduce the amount of Drag and/or Weight?

Organizational leaders should include the improvement cycle in their change management plans to avoid burnout.

It is allowable to descend an organization to a lower altitude, but leaders must not allow the organization to stay at the lower altitude.

Landing is the most difficult maneuver to accomplish whether it's an airplane, organization, or life.

Epilogue/Conclusion

To attain success, three key forces must be in harmony: Energy, Motivation, and a Supportive Environment. Any deficiency in either one will delay or even curtail your efforts to achieve success. Think of a returning war veteran who is an amputee. The military can provide the best supportive environment at Walter Reed Hospital but if the person lacks the energy or the motivation due to depression, very little can be accomplished. On the other hand, if that wounded warrior is both energetic and motivated but does not have a facility with the right equipment for rehabilitation, their progress may be much slower. These three forces are analogous to the aeronautical forces that pilots and aviators encounter in flight operations. To move an airplane forward, the pilots must use energy, also known as Thrust in aviation terms, to overcome the force of Drag. If Thrust is greater than Drag, the aircraft moves forward. As an aircraft moves forward, the wind sweeps over the wing to create the force of Lift. Lift is what takes the aircraft into the atmosphere for flight and is analogous to the motivation that is required for you to achieve your goals. Regardless of the goal being personal or organizational, it takes energy to produce motivation and a supportive environment in which to operate to bring it all together. Just like an aviator in an aircraft requires all three to be in harmony to safely execute their mission.

Aviators use situational awareness to recognize the forces that are impeding their progress, and they adjust and maneuver to keep their aircraft flying. You must do the same. For example, once you become aware of the induced or parasitic Drag that is draining the energy from your people, you must reduce or eliminate it, so the team has the energy to take your organization to the next level. Pilots do the same when they Lift the landing gear after takeoff so the aircraft can continue climbing. The force of Lift must be greater than both Drag and Weight for an aircraft to climb to a higher altitude. You need motivation to overcome the Weight that keeps you grounded. The past mistakes, the self-doubt, and the fear that weighs you down. Only through motivation or Lifting of your spirits do you press forward despite the fears and doubt. Finally, once you have the energy and the motivation, you must find a supportive environment in which to fly. It may mean changing jobs, changing the company's value proposition, or changing the community in which you live. Regardless of what changes, you must allow for the energies and motivations expressed earlier to flourish. That's when you and your organization can reach the stratosphere where turbulence becomes less of a factor, and you can become "Too Big to Fail".

Bibliography

Dusenbury, M, Balogh, S. and Ullrich, G. (2016, August 9). *Aerodynamics for Aviators*. Aviation Supplies & Academics, Inc. Kindle Edition.

Cutter, C. and Cameron, D. (2020, July 19). U.S. Companies Lose Hope for Quick Rebound From Covid-19. *Wall Street Journal*. Retrieved from https://www.wsj.com/articles/u-s-companies-lose-hope-for-quick-rebound-from-covid-19-11595151000

Hari, J. (2022, January 25). Stolen Focus: Why You Can't Pay Attention and How to Think Deeply Again. Crown. ISBN 059338511

Huff, S. (2019, September 26). Classic 80s-Era Wine Coolers Bartles & Jaymes Are Making a Comeback. *Maxim*. Retrieved from https://www.maxim.com/food-drink/80s-wine-cooler-maker-bartles-jaymes-comeback-2019-9

Nolen, J. (2021, June 17). Ursula Burns: American Executive. *Britannica*. Retrieved from https://www.britannica.com/biography/Ursula-Burns

Switzer, Barry. *Quotetab*. Retrieved from https://www.quotetab.com/quotes/by-barry-switzer

Zetlin, M. (2020, September 20). Blockbuster Could Have Bought Netflix for $50 Million, but the CEO Thought It Was a Joke. *Inc*. Retrieved from https://www.inc.com/minda-zetlin/netflix-blockbuster-meeting-marc-randolph-reed-hastings-john-antioco.html

Elliot-Moskwa, E. (2022). *The Growth Mindset Workbook: CBT Skills to Help You Build Resilience, Increase Confidence & Thrive through Life's Challenges*. New Harbinger Publications, Inc. Kindle Edition.

Acknowledgments

I am grateful to the numerous individuals who have contributed their time and talents to the creation of this book. My family deserves special recognition for their unwavering support and willingness to serve as a sounding board for my ideas. Their honest, tough, and invaluable feedback has been essential to the development of this project. I also extend a huge thank you to the gifted illustrator, Lizzy Ferris, whose exceptional sketches were produced within a tight timeframe.

Your remarkable artistic abilities continue to impress me, and I hope you will continue to hone your talents. Lastly, I would like to express my appreciation to the courageous aviators who shared many long nights with me, soaring high above the earth. To the Air Commandos who have played a significant role in shaping the leader I am today, I am forever indebted. You instilled in me the value of humility and the importance of being a silent warrior who takes pride in accomplishing the mission with precision and excellence.

I want to thank my fellow Rotarians for sharing their stories with me. Jeff Blum, Lissa Kreisler, Marty Fishman, Haryl Pascal, and Erik Van der Burg. Finally, a special shout out to my coach's coach, Rick Franzo, for sharing his book, <u>How Horseshoes Saved My Life: A Tale of Two Brain Tumors</u>. Your story is inspirational and shows the strength of the human spirit. May you continue to inspire others for a long time.

About the Author

Ramon Ware's journey as a leader began during his studies at The United States Air Force Academy, one of the largest leadership laboratories in America. He completed his Bachelor of Science degree with a major in Behavioral Science and served as a navigator rated aviator for over nine years on Special Operations MC-130 aircraft while on active duty. Ramon then embarked on a corporate career that spanned over 20 years, where he climbed the ranks to executive leadership positions. During this time, he also worked part-time as an adjunct professor at several colleges and universities. After leaving corporate America, Ramon purchased a franchise with The Growth Coach and now operates as The Growth Coach of San Jose South in California. Ramon is married with six adult children and one granddaughter, and he enjoys traveling with his wife and fishing whenever possible.

Made in the USA
Middletown, DE
09 December 2023

45070705R00116